WHERE I LIVE

On an Island

Fiona Macdonald

WAYLAND

Explore the world with **Popcorn** - your complete first non-fiction library.

Look out for more titles in the Popcorn range. All books have the same format of simple text and striking images. Text is carefully matched to the pictures to help readers to identify and understand key vocabulary.
www.waylandbooks.co.uk/popcorn

First published in 2010 by Wayland
Copyright © Wayland 2010

Wayland
Hachette Children's Books
338 Euston Road
London NW1 3BH

Wayland Australia
Level 17/207 Kent Street
Sydney NSW 2000

Produced for Wayland by
White-Thomson Publishing Ltd
www.wtpub.co.uk
+44 (0)843 208 7460

Editor: Steve White-Thomson
Designer: Clare Nicholas
Series consultant: Kate Ruttle
Commissioned photography: Tony Oliver
Design concept: Paul Cherrill

British Library Cataloging in Publication Data
Macdonald, Fiona, 1958-
   On an island. -- (Popcorn. Where I live)
   1. Coll Island (Scotland)--Pictorial works--Juvenile
   literature.
   I. Title II. Series
   941.1'54-dc22

ISBN: 978 0 7502 6317 7

Wayland is a division of Hachette Children's Books,
an Hachette UK company.
www.hachette.co.uk

Printed and bound in China

Fiona Macdonald would like to give very special thanks to the Pupils and Head Teacher of Arinagour Primary School, Coll, for their warm welcome and for all the help, advice and information they most generously provided. The publishers would also like to thank Lexi, her sisters - Polly and Grace - and her parents Doug and Catriona Young, and Tony Oliver for his excellent photographs.

 Contents

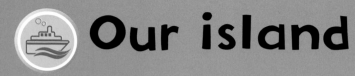

Our island

My name is Lexi. I live on an island called Coll, in Scotland. The island is small and rocky.

Creels are used for catching crab, prawns and lobsters.

4

About 180 adults and 50 children live on the island. It is a friendly place. We all know each other!

This is my family and our house.

The island measures about 19 km long and 5 km wide.

Rocks and beaches

The island is surrounded by sea. Sometimes the sea is rough, with huge, dangerous waves. Sometimes it is calm and then it's safe for swimming.

I'm dancing in the sea!

Crash! A monster wave smashes against rocks on the shore.

There are steep cliffs, rock pools, shells, seaweed and beautiful sandy beaches. We like to build sandcastles.

This is North Beach. The sea is cold and clear.

The village

The island has one main village.
About half the islanders live there.
The rest live in the countryside.

The village is called Arinagour
(say:Arr-in-ah-gow-er).

top of hotel   main pier   Island cafe

The village has the only shops on the island. There is a post office, a general store with petrol pumps, a cafe and a pottery. There is a village taxi, but no buses or trains.

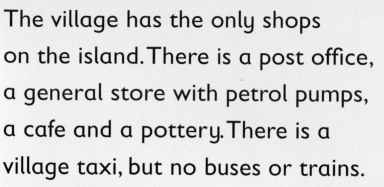

There are only two roads on the island.

This is the village church. There is also a village hall and a doctor's surgery.

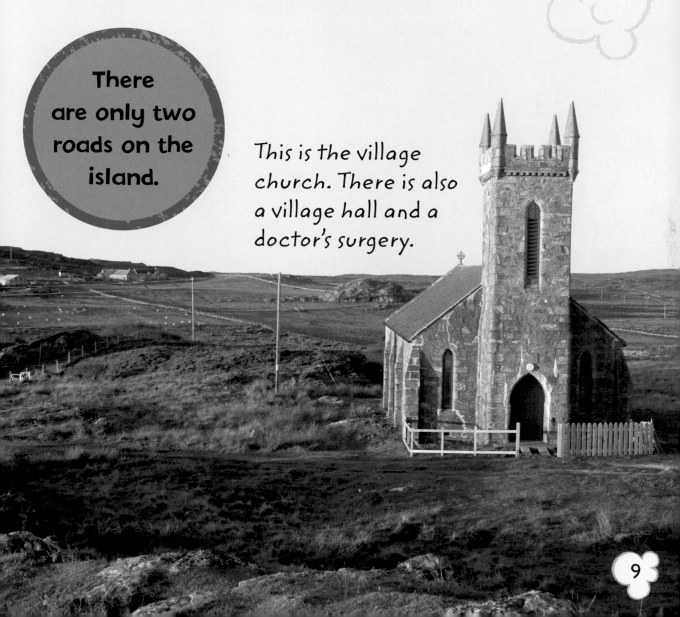

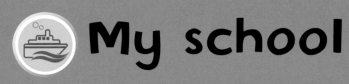 My school

Most of us walk or cycle to school.
Older children go to boarding school
on the mainland. They come home for
weekends and in the holidays.

This is me, with some friends, in our school uniform.

In class, we read, write, paint, do maths and learn to speak French and Gaelic. We do PE in the field outside our classroom or the village hall.

Gaelic (say Gall-ick) is a language spoken in the north and west of Scotland, and on many Scottish islands.

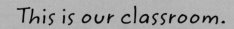

This is our classroom.

Ferries and planes

We travel to and from the island by ferry and by plane. It takes about 3 hours by ferry to reach the mainland. The ferry brings fresh milk, bread and newspapers.

Ferries dock at the main pier.

When the weather is stormy, ferries and planes cannot reach the island. We are cut off from the rest of the world!

The island ambulance is a helicopter. It takes people to hospital on the mainland.

Planes land on the airstrip.

Summer visitors

Many tourists visit the island in summertime. They go walking and cycling. They admire the scenery and the historic buildings.

There is an old castle (left) and a newer castle on the island.

Visitors stay at the hotel or the campsite, or have bed and breakfast in islanders' houses. They enjoy the peace and quiet, and the clean, fresh air.

In summer, the hotel is always busy.

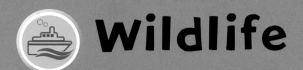

Wildlife

Many people come to the island to watch birds. Huge eagles and rare birds called corncrakes live here. There is a big nature reserve on the island.

Corncrakes make an amazing noise: 'Crex, Crex, Crex'.

Unlike most other birds, corncrakes sing all night long.

Other visitors go on boat-trips
to look for seals, whales, dolphins
and basking sharks. They study
seashells, rocks and wild flowers.

Otters hunt fish and leave
tracks on the beaches.

Working together

Some islanders are farmers.
Some catch fish from the sea.
Some are artists or writers,
or work with computers.

Fishermen bring
their catch
safely home
to the island.

People on the island also help the community. They raise money for good causes. They volunteer to be coastguards or firefighters.

Putting out a fire on the island.

Volunteers are people who help, without pay.

Having fun

In summer, we go camping, sailing or play golf. In winter, we play music on fiddles and drums, learn Scottish dancing and enjoy ceilidhs.

At ceilidhs (say: kay-leez) there is music and dancing. People tell stories and jokes.

We love bodyboarding in summertime.

We also have fun at community events. We put on fancy dress for the Garden Party, run in the Children's Race and enter competitions at the Summer Show.

Will they win the tug-of-war at the Summer Show?

Island quiz

Test your knowledge of life on the island of Coll. How much can you remember?

1 What noise does this bird make?

2 Where does this boat sail to?

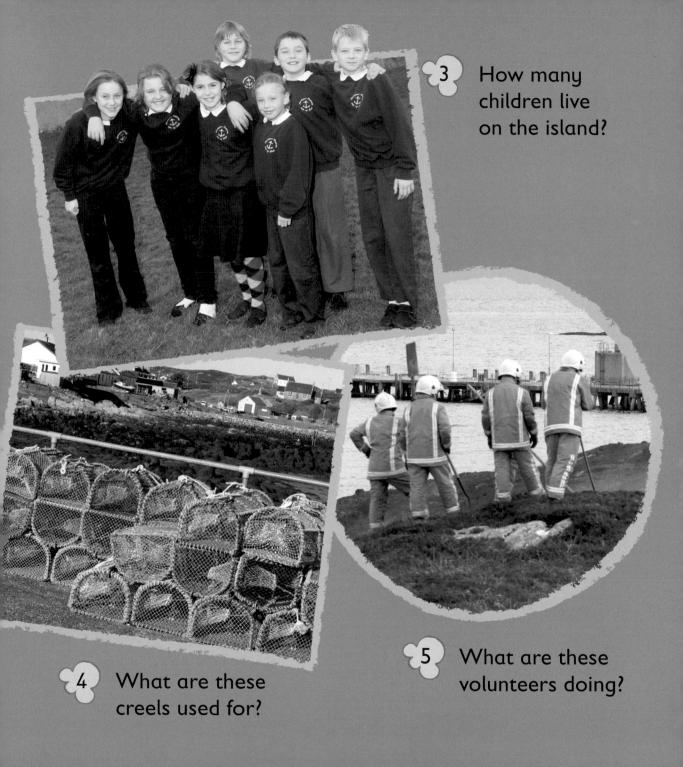

3 How many children live on the island?

4 What are these creels used for?

5 What are these volunteers doing?

1: Crex, Crex, Crex. 2: From the mainland to the island. 3: About 50. 4: Catching crabs, prawns and lobsters. 5: Helping to put out a fire.

23

Glossary

basking shark a huge fish, almost 10 metres long

boarding schools where pupils live during term-time

coastguards people who help sailors and swimmers stay safe

creel underwater trap, made of metal and net, used to catch sea creatures

ferry a boat that makes regular trips to carry people, cars, food, fuel and other essential items

islanders people who live on an island

mainland land nearest to an island

nature reserve a safe place for wildlife

Index

Where I Live

Contents of titles in the series:

WAYLAND